D0831521

For a Righteous Man

Presented By

Prayers
of a
Righteous Man

Jim Gallery

BB

Brighton Books
Nashville, TN

Prayers

of a

Righteous Man

Jim Gallery

ISBN 1-58334-110-2

The quoted ideas expressed in this book (but not scripture verses) are not, in all cases, exact quotations, as some have been edited for clarity and brevity. In all cases, the author has attempted to maintain the speaker's original intent. In some cases, quoted material for this book was obtained from secondary sources, primarily print media. While every effort was made to ensure the accuracy of these sources, the accuracy cannot be guaranteed. For additions, deletions, corrections or clarifications in future editions of this text, please write BRIGHTON BOOKS.

Printed in the United States of America
Cover Design & Page Layout: *Bart Dawson*

1 2 3 4 5 6 7 8 9 10 • 01 02 03 04 05 06 07 08 09 10

Acknowledgments: The author is indebted to Criswell Freeman for his support and friendship and the helpful staff at Walnut Grove Press.

In dedication to:

Floyd Price, A Dear Friend
and
A Righteous Man

Table of Contents

Help me, Lord:

How to Use This Book

Daily life is a tapestry woven together by the threads of habit. Our habits determine, in large part, who we are and who we become. If we develop habits that enrich our lives and the lives of others, we are blessed by God. If, on the other hand, we fall prey to negative thoughts or destructive behavior, we suffer.

No habit is more important to your life than the habit of daily devotion and prayer. God calls upon each of us to worship him with a thankful heart, and He instructs us to pray without ceasing. But amid the hustle and bustle of the daily grind, prayer and thanksgiving are too often neglected, even by those who know and love God.

This little book is intended as a tool for men as they develop and reinforce the habit of daily meditation and prayer. As such, the book is divided into 31 chapters, one for each day of the month. During the next 31 days, please try this experiment: read a chapter each day. If you're already committed to a daily worship time, this book will enrich that experience. If you are not, the simple act of giving God a few minutes each morning will change the tone and direction of your life.

Whether you work with your hands or manage a Fortune 500 company, whether you wear a blue-collar or a white one, whether you are the breadwinner or Mr. Mom, you need a daily conference with God. So why not make it a habit to talk things over with Him each day? When you do, your life will become more joyful, more peaceful, and more abundant.

"The prayer of a righteous man is
                powerful and effective."

James 5:16b

Introduction

A wise man desires a life of significance. To that end, he seeks meaningful work and fulfilling relationships. To that end, he safeguards his physical health, his mental health, and above all, his spiritual health. A wise man understands that the blessings of this life—and the next—are always found in the presence of God. And he understands that God's presence is encountered in the act of prayer.

The Creator and Sustainer of life is the same Being that gives significance and meaning to life. When man turns his eyes and heart toward heaven for instruction, God never fails to deliver the road map.

The righteous man seeks God in church and beyond; most importantly, he seeks God through prayer. The pages that follow contain quotations, stories, prayers, and Bible verses that demonstrate the power of prayer, the importance of prayer, and the necessity for prayer. These pages are intended to assist any man who sincerely desires to live an upright, significant, Godly life. That life begins—and ends—and begins anew—with God's gift of prayer.

15

"Commit to the Lord whatever you do,
and your plans will succeed."

Proverbs 16:3

Help Me, Lord...

To Reflect
Your Love

> "So God created man in his image,
> in the image of God he created him…"
>
> *Genesis 1:27*
>
> "…God is love…"
>
> *1 John 4:16*

The bumper sticker makes the point:

We are not human beings with spiritual concerns.
We are spiritual beings with human concerns.

God created man in His image to be a reflection of His character in the world.

God is truth...thus, man is to reflect God's truth.

God is caring...thus, man is to reflect God's caring.

God is love...thus, man is to reflect God's love.

The Apostle Paul writes that man has been reconciled to God through Jesus Christ. Man is given a ministry of reconciliation, and he is used by God to bring others to Christ. Paul calls these righteous men ambassadors because they represent the King and go out in His power and with His blessing.

The story is told of a young orphan boy in a third world country. He was dirty, dressed in tattered clothing, hungry, and forlorn. As the boy passed by a bakery, tempting pastries and a wonderful aroma stopped him in his tracks. He pressed his face against the window and longed for a taste.

Inside the bakery, an American soldier was buying rolls when he noticed the young boy gazing through the window. As the soldier left the bakery, he handed the lad a pastry, wished him well, and walked on. Soon, the soldier felt a tug on his pant leg. It was the same young boy who, with a slightly puzzled look, asked a simple question: "Hey mister, are you God?"

The answer, of course, was no, the soldier was not God. But the soldier was an ambassador for God as he cared for that young boy. The righteous man knows that in all he says and does, he represents God to a world in need.

"Putting on Christ"…is not one among many jobs
a Christian has to do; and it is not a sort of
special exercise for the top class. It is
the whole of Christianity.
Christianity offers nothing else at all.

C.S. Lewis

Make it a rule and pray to God to help you to
keep it, never, if possible, to lie down at night
without being able to say: "I have made one human
being at least a little wiser, or a little happier, or at
least a little better this day."

Charles Kingsley

Preach the gospel at all times and,
if necessary, use words.

St. Francis of Assisi

22

The Gospel According to Me

Help me remember when others I see;
That they're reading the gospel according to me.
Matthew and Barnabus and Peter and Paul—
The world looks upon them as names—that's all.

For the verses of scripture, lost men merely grope.
But my life goes under the microscope.
Make me a text, Lord, easy to read—
When men read the gospel according to me.

Anonymous

Today's Prayer

*L*ord, help me to be an example of
Your love and Your truth to everyone I meet.
Help me to always be mindful that my life
can be—and should be—a living testimony to
Your grace and your redemption. And let me always
follow Your will as I seek to share the healing
message of Your Son, this day and every day.

Amen

2

Help Me, Lord...
To Live by the
Truth of Your Word

"He humbled you, causing you to hunger
and then feeding you manna, which
neither you nor your fathers had known,
to teach you that man does not live by
bread alone but on every word that
comes from the mouth of the LORD."

Deuteronomy 8:3

In his book, In The Eye Of The Storm, *Max Lucado shares a story illustrating the fact that absolute truths can't be changed. Lucado writes of a battleship maneuvering at night in rough seas. Through the fog, the battleship's captain saw a distant but approaching light. He instructed the signalman to alert the approaching ship to change course in order to avoid a collision. But the response to the captain's signal was surprising: It advised the battleship to change course. At first, the captain was slightly peeved, so he signaled back with this message: "I am a captain, change course." But again, the response to the captain's orders was surprising: "Sir, I am a signalman and a seaman 2nd class, and you still need to change course." The captain, by now irate, flashed a final warning: "We are a battleship." The response was equally terse: "We are a lighthouse." The battleship changed course.*

God's Word is our lighthouse in the turbulent seas of life. The righteous man knows that unchanging truth is found in God.

God did not write a book and send it by messenger
to be read at a distance by unaided minds.
He spoke a Book and lives in His spoken words,
constantly speaking His words and causing the
power of them to persist across the years.

A.W. Tozer

The Bible is God's Word, given to us by God Himself
so we can know Him and His will for our lives.

Billy Graham

Nobody ever outgrows Scripture;
the book widens and deepens with our years.

C.H. Spurgeon

I am a creature of a day. I am a spirit come from
God, and returning to God. I want to know one
thing: the way to heaven. God himself has
condescended to teach me the way. He has
written it down in a book. Oh, give me that book!
At any price give me the book of God.
Let me be a man of one book.

John Wesley

Today's Prayer

*L*ord, keep me focused on You
and Your truth. Do not let me be intimidated
by the worldly wisdom of man. Mankind's wisdom
is of this world. Your truth, Lord, is found in
Your word. It is absolute. May I be a voice of
Your truth, unwavering and sure.

Amen

Help Me, Lord...

To Be a Man After Your Own Heart

"...the LORD has sought out a man
after his own heart and appointed him
leader of his people..."

1 Samuel 13:14

The Bible tells us that David was a man after God's own heart. God honored and blessed this king who loved Him so. David's love for God was not perfect, and he made grievous mistakes, but his heart kept bringing him back to God.

When the prophet Samuel enlightened David concerning his terrible sin of adultery with Bathsheba and the murder of her husband Uriah, David's heart would not give him peace until he sought forgiveness from God. David cried, "Create in me a clean heart, O God" *(Psalm 51:10a)*.

The righteous man is not perfect. But the righteous man *desires* perfection and seeks to correct his errors by making amends for his wrongdoing.

Our Father, we are beginning to understand at last
that the things that are wrong with our world
are the sum total of all the things that are wrong
with us as individuals. Thou hast made us after
Thine image, and our hearts can find no rest until
they rest in Thee.

Peter Marshall

Whether we think of, or speak to, God, whether
we act or suffer for him, all is prayer, when we
have no other object than his love, and the
desire of pleasing him.

John Wesley

Our Savior kneels down and gazes upon the
darkest acts of our lives. But rather than recoil
in horror, he reaches out in kindness and says,
"I can clean that if you want." And from the
basin of his grace, he scoops a palm full of mercy
and washes our sin.

Max Lucado

Today's Prayer

*L*ord, help me to be
wholly committed to You.
May my heart beat for You, and
may I be filled with Your righteousness.
When I fall short, Lord, show me the
error of my ways. Let me be a man after
Your heart, God, and let me seek
Your perfect will, this day and always.

Amen

$\mathscr{H}elp$ $\mathscr{M}e,$ $\mathscr{L}ord...$

To See Things from Your Perspective

"When I consider your heavens, the work of
your fingers, the moon and the stars,
which you have set in place, what is man
that your are mindful of him, the son of man
that you care for him? You made him a little
lower than the heavenly beings and crowned
him with glory and honor. You made him
ruler over the works of your hands; you put
everything under his feet: all flocks and herds,
and the beasts of the field, and the birds of
the air, and the fish of the sea, all that swim
the paths of the seas."

Psalm 8:3-8

W*hile hiking on the Appalachian Trail, we spent nights in enclosed lean-tos, and for good reason: hungry bears. Usually, Smokey Mountain bears are satisfied to dine on an occasional backpack or two, but on rare occasions, they prefer the proprietors of the backpacks, so we were cautious.*

O*ne morning, after sleeping on the wire cots in an enclosed lean-to, my fellow hikers and I were enjoying breakfast when we observed a four-legged visitor rumbling down the path. The brown bear didn't seem too threatening, but we were in no mood to take risks, so we beat a hasty retreat into the lean-to. All of us, that is, except David. David wanted photographs to forever memorialize our brush with danger, so he pulled out his small camera and started clicking. As the bear came closer and closer, David stood, still as a statue, clicking and winding, clicking and winding, clicking and winding, never taking his eye off the camera's tiny lens. Gradually, we came to realize that David saw a different bear through his undersized viewfinder. In David's mind, the bear was still far away, but in reality, it had ambled within an easy paw's reach of our daring (dare I say foolhardy?) friend.*

O*ur cries of warning finally caused David to lower his camera. Immediately, he realized that the bear was not just close, but very close. David quickly jumped out of harm's way and slammed the lean-to door. And I learned a lesson on perspective: David's perspective, the one provided through the lens of his small camera, was not reality. The same can be said for the ways that we sometimes view life.*

Sometimes, the world seems to be in focus, but it's not. Sometimes, we think that we share God's perspective, but we don't. Like my friend David looking through his viewfinder, we believe things to be a certain way, but reality is different, indeed.

When we live for God, we are blessed by Him. When we live for God, we see the world through His perspective, and we behave in accordance with His plan no matter what others may think or say. God's perspective is reality. Everything else is illusion.

We need never shout across the spaces to an
    absent God. He is nearer than our own
    soul, closer than our most secret thoughts.

A.W. Tozer

God walks with us. . . . He scoops us up in His arms
    or simply sits with us in silent strength until
    we cannot avoid the awesome recognition
    that yes, even now, He is there.

Gloria Gaither

Today's Prayer

*L*ord, help me to see the world through
your eyes. Sometimes, the world's perspective
can be dangerous to my well-being. May I always
seek to interpret my circumstances and
relationships through the truth of Your word.
Give me guidance, Lord, and wisdom.
Lead me according to Your plan for my life,
and keep me ever-mindful that Your reality is
the ultimate reality, and that Your truth is
the ultimate truth, now and forever.

Amen

5

Help Me, Lord...
To Be
Wholly Committed
To My Wife

"...For this reason a man will leave his
father and mother and be united to his
wife, and the two will become one flesh.
So they are no longer two, but one.
Therefore what God has joined together
let no man separate."

Matthew 19:5,6

I gift my children with my hard work;
I gift my children with my time;
I gift my children with affirming words;
I gift my children with hugs of affection;
But I gift my children best by loving my wife,
their mother.

The first essential for a happy home is love.

Billy Graham

The acid test of a father's leadership is not in the
realm of his social skills, his public relations,
his managerial abilities at the office, or how
well he handles himself before the public.
It is in the home.

Chuck Swindoll

It is a reverent thing to see an ancient castle or
building not in decay, or to see a fair timber tree
sound and perfect. How much more to behold an
ancient and noble family that has stood against the
waves and weathers of time.

Francis Bacon

Today's Prayer

*L*ord, there are many good things that
demand my time: my family, my friends,
my work, my play, and a multitude of concerns
that slowly and surely gobble up the hours of
my day. Help me Lord to always remember
how precious is the love of my wife. May I love
her as Christ loved His church, and may I
cherish her and protect her and encourage her
and praise her today and every day.

Amen

Help Me, Lord...

To Have
The Right Priorities

"What good is it for a man to gain the
whole world, yet forfeit his soul?"

Mark 8:36

Should a growing relationship with God be the most important priority of life? Thoughtful Christians respond in the affirmative. And how can we cultivate a relationship with God? By spending time with Him.

Most of us have been guilty of saying, "There are not enough hours in a day," but we are mistaken. God made enough hours in the day for the important things, but He didn't make enough hours in the day for everything. God's day is long enough if we use it well.

Many voices cry out to us wanting and, sometimes, demanding our attention. Jesus has a word of advice for us as we try to get it all done: "Seek first his kingdom and his righteousness, and all these things will be given to you as well." (Matthew 6:33) If we learn to put first things first, everything else falls into place. And for Christians, the first thing, now and always, is making time for God.

As is the business of tailors to make clothes and cobblers to make shoes, so it is the business of Christians to pray.

Martin Luther

The moment you wake up each morning, all your wishes and hopes for the day rush at you like wild animals. And the first job each morning consists in shoving it all back; in listening to that other voice, taking that other point of view, letting that other, larger, stronger, quieter life come flowing in.

C.S. Lewis

O, let the place of secret prayer become to me the most beloved spot on earth.

Andrew Murray

Today's Prayer

*L*ord, I want to be a man who is focused
on the important things of life. Help me
not to be overwhelmed by the urgent
things of life. Lord, let my spiritual life be
ever-growing, and give me the perspective
to see Your purpose for me more clearly
each day as I spend time in quiet reflection
on Your Word and Your will.

Amen

Help Me, Lord...
To Grow In You

"When I was a child, I talked like a
child, I thought like a child, I reasoned
like a child. When I became a man, I
put childish ways behind me."

I Cor 13:11

There are some childlike traits that are admirable. In fact, Jesus says that to enter the kingdom of God one must become childlike: "...Let the little children come to me, and do not hinder them, for the kingdom of God belongs to such as these." (Mark 10:14)

But the righteous man is to put away childish things. Paul writes in Hebrews that some Christians who should be making and teaching disciples are still learning the ABCs of their faith. He warns that immature Christians do not grow spiritually, and because of their lack of growth, the work of the kingdom suffers: "...though by this time you ought to be teachers, you need someone to teach you the elementary truths of God's word all over again." (5:12)

Let us therefore be childlike in our love and enthusiasm for Christ, but let us also be mature in our willingness to embrace spiritual growth as we share the Good News of Jesus.

Often God shuts a door in our face so that he can
open the door through which he wants us to go.

Catherine Marshall

I've never met anyone who became instantly mature.
It's a painstaking process that God takes
us through, and it includes such things as waiting,
failing, losing, and being misunderstood —
each calling for extra doses of perseverance.

Charles Swindol

We should not be upset when unexpected and
upsetting things happen. God in his wisdom
means to make something of us which we
have not yet attained and is dealing
with us accordingly.

J.I. Packer

God loves us the way we are, but
He loves us too much to leave us that way.

Leighton Ford

47

Today's Prayer

*L*ord, the work of Your kingdom
suffers if I don't take my place as a mature
Christian. Help me to walk along a path of
spiritual growth, trusting in Your way and
Your Word, learning each day to love
You more and to do Your will.

Amen

Help Me, Lord...
To Love Others

"And a new command I give you: Love one another. As I have loved you, so you must love one another. By this all men will know that you are my disciples, if you love one another."

John 13:34,35

Good works, church attendance, tithing, and talking about Jesus are all good ways to show our commitment to Christ. But Jesus says the best way for the world to know those who belong to Him is by the love they show to one another.

John writes that someone with God's love will: Lay down his life for his brother; Give his material possessions to a needy brother; Do things to express the love he talks about (1 John 3:16-18).

For days I had been listening to the PhDs tell me the best way for my child to learn. Some of these well-meaning educators spoke with compassion while others were matter-of-fact to the point of coldness. I began questioning my beliefs on what was best for my son in the midst of these high-powered, educated men and women. As I sat through yet another meeting, it suddenly dawned on me: There was only one person in that room who was willing to lay his life down for my son...me. No longer was I intimidated. My love for my son superseded the concern of others because I was willing to sacrifice everything for him.

Jesus says that in a world dominated by self-interest, some people will demonstrate selfless love for one another. They are called Christians...followers of Christ.

Our prayer must not be self-centered. It must
arise not only because we feel our own need as a
burden we must lay upon God, but also because
we are so bound up in love for our fellow men
that we feel their need as acutely as our own.
To make intercession for men is the most
powerful and practical way in which we can express
our love for them.

John Calvin

The whole being of any Christian is Faith and
Love.... Faith brings the man to God,
love brings him to men.

Martin Luther

An ounce of love is worth a pound of knowledge.

John Wesley

51

Today's Prayer

*L*ord, I want those I meet to know
I am your disciple. May my love for
others be evident and expressive so that
others may see Your love reflected in my actions.
I am your follower, Lord. Help me always
to follow your commandment to love your
children as You have loved me.

Amen

Help Me, Lord...

To Be a
Witness for You

"Come, follow me, and I will make you
fishers of men."

Matthew 4:19

When we lose our focus on the priorities of life, bad things happen. The gospels all begin with Jesus saying, "Come and follow." They end with Jesus commanding his disciples to "Go and tell." The righteous man has the objective in life to fulfil the Great Commission: "…go and make disciples of all nations, baptizing them in the name of the Father and of the Son and of the Holy Spirit, and teaching them to obey everything I have commanded you…." *(Matthew 28:19-20)* Jesus called it "fishing for men."

A group of Christian builders came to help construct our new sanctuary. Our congregation was blessed by their generosity. The men were especially excited about their pastor's visit on Wednesday to help with the construction and to share his "fishing sermon" that night.

The pastor told of going fishing with some buddies in the late fall. Each day, the weather worsened. Instead of fishing, the men were forced to entertain each other. It seems the weather wasn't the only thing that worsened each day. The pastor reported of growing testiness between the men until, finally, everyone packed up and went home. The pastor's punch line was powerful and to the point: "When fisherman don't fish, they fight."

The pastor's story makes an important point: When the purpose of a trip is to fish, and when fishing doesn't take

54

---

place, frustration and fussing and fighting are likely to occur. But, when individuals or groups stay on target, fulfillment and satisfaction result (with a side benefit: harmony). The righteous man stays focused on the great calling: to be a witness for Christ and a servant to others.

No man is ever the same after God has
laid His hand upon him.

A.W. Tozer

Christ's work of making new men...
is not mere improvement, but transformation.

C.S. Lewis

Taking the gospel to people wherever they are—
death row, the ghetto, or next door—is frontline
evangelism. Frontline love. It is our one hope
for breaking down barriers and for restoring
the sense of community.

Charles Colson

Today's Prayer

*L*ord, I want to follow you and be a
fisher of men. When I feel unfulfilled and
unfocused, remind of my purpose. In all that I do,
help me be a worthy witness for You to a
world that so desperately needs
Your saving grace.

Amen

Help Me, Lord...

To Be an
Example of Good

> "...let your light shine before men, that they may see your good deeds and praise your Father in heaven."
>
> *Matthew 5:16*

As a part of my first ministry duties after seminary, I served as a youth pastor at a large church. I'll never forget the senior pastor's charge to me for ministering to the youth. He challenged me to "draw the young people to you and point them to God." But I was puzzled: Why not just point them to God and forget about "me"? It wasn't long before I understood the wisdom of the pastor's words. He understood that the youth needed not only my words but also my friendship, my encouragement, and my example.

God sent 'The Word", His son Jesus, to live among us. Jesus was fully divine, and He was fully human. Jesus is mankind's example of righteousness on earth. Jesus gives His children love, encouragement, and salvation. His example is perfect. May each of us follow His teachings, and, to the best of our abilities, His example as we share His message.

Lord, I am no longer my own, but Yours.
Put me to what You will, rank me with whom
You will. Let be employed by You or laid aside for
You, exalted for You or brought low by You.
Let me have all things, let me have nothing,
I freely and heartily yield all things to Your pleasure
and disposal. And now, O glorious and blessed
God, Father, Son, and Holy Spirit, You are mine
and I am Yours. So be it. Amen.

John Wesley

The wise Christian will watch for opportunities to
do good, to speak the life-bringing word to sinners,
to pray the rescuing prayer of intercession.

A.W. Tozer

Don't worry about what you do not understand.
Worry about what you do understand in the
Bible but do not live by.

Corrie ten Boom

Today's Prayer

*L*ord, You deserve all praise, honor, and glory.
You have chosen me as a tool to minister
to others. May I be an example of godly living
to everyone I meet. Help me, Lord, always to
share Your joy with others through my
words and my deeds.

Amen

Help Me, Lord...
To Obey You

"Peter and the other apostles replied:
'We must obey God
rather than men!'"

Acts 5:29

Peter and the apostles were healing the sick and the demon-possessed. They were performing miracles. And they were upsetting the religious leaders of the day who felt threatened by the large number of men and women who were becoming Christians. The apostles were ordered never to preach the Good News of Jesus, but they did. So Peter and the apostles were thrown into jail where an angel promptly set them free. Then, the apostles were brought before the Sanhedrin and chastised by the high priest: "We gave you strict orders not to teach in this name…yet you have filled Jerusalem with your teaching and are determined to make us guilty of this man's blood."*(Acts 5:28)* Peter and the apostles were not intimidated. They knew that they must obey God and not men.

As a child I was intrigued with the fiery furnace of the Shadrach, Meshach, and Abednego story. As an adult, I am captivated by the three boys and their resolve to obey God no matter what. The boys refused to follow the king's decree and bow down to his image, so they were given a lecture by King Nebuchadnezzar himself. If they failed to comply with the king's wishes, the fiery furnace awaited them.

Shadrach, Meshach, and Abednego responded, "…O Nebuchadnezzar, we do not need to defend ourselves before you in this matter. If we are thrown into the blazing furnace, the God we serve is able to save us from it, and he will rescue us from it, and he will rescue us from you hand, O king. But even if he does not, we want you to know, O king, that we will not serve your gods or worship the image of god you have set up." (Daniel 3:16-18) The three young men obeyed God, not man, and we must do likewise.

It is one thing to love the ways of the Lord when
all is well and quite another thing to cling to them
during discouragement or difficulty.

C. H. Spurgeon

From the tiny birds of the air and from the fragile
lilies of the field, we learn the same truth:
God takes care of His own. At just the right
moment, He steps in and proves Himself as our
faithful heavenly Father.

Charles Swindol

When we choose deliberately to obey Him,
then He will tax the remotest star and the
last grain of sand to assist us with all
His almighty power.

Oswald Chambers

Today's Prayer

*L*ord, perhaps I will never face a
choice between You and a fiery furnace.
But Lord, each day, I face choices between
Your way and the world's way. Help me
always to make wise decisions. May I,
like Joshua, choose this day to follow You.

Amen

Help Me, Lord...
To Know the Freedom of Truthful Living

"You shall know the truth and the truth shall set you free"

John 8:32

Freedom is a precious thing. We desire the freedom to pursue happiness and to freedom to pursue our goals. But freedom is also paradoxical in that we are never truly free until we place ourselves in bondage to the true and living God.

Jesus said, "I am the way and the truth and the life. No one comes to the Father except through me" *(John 14:6)* Following Jesus and committing one's life to Him is the door to genuine freedom. The pursuit of freedom in any other form is, in fact, a form of imprisonment which God never intended.

Peace, if possible, but truth at any rate.

Martin Luther

A little lie is like a little pregnancy it
    doesn't take long before everyone knows.

C.S. Lewis

I would rather know the truth than be happy
    in ignorance. If I cannot have both truth and
happiness, give me truth. We'll have a long time to
        be happy in heaven.

A.W. Tozer

Today's Prayer

*L*ord, help me always to understand
that my freedom lies in Your will. Your Son
Jesus is the salvation of the world. His way is
the path of truth and everlasting life.
Help me always to walk on His path
and live in His light.

Amen

Help Me, Lord...
To Please You

"...We are not trying to please men,
but God..."

I Thessalonians 2:4b

*O*ur high school basketball team needed help, and our principal knew it. So he went all the way from Florida to Indiana, the hotbed of basketball, to secure the services of one Hugh Thimler. Coach Thimler promptly turned our team's basketball fortunes in the right direction. Coach Thimler taught us about basketball and life, but not necessarily in that order.

*B*efore Thimler arrived, our team had begun to develop a "run and gun" offense, but Coach wanted a more deliberate style of play. He instituted a rule that we must pass the ball at least three times before any shot was taken. In the first game after the rule took effect, Andy Torgenson brought the ball down court and passed to me. Even though, according to Coach Thimler, I should have passed the ball, I felt I was too open to miss the 30-foot shot. I took the shot and made it. The fans cheered, and the cheerleaders were duly impressed. Coach Thimler was not. He called time-out and pulled me from the game. I sat me on the bench for the rest of the game.

I quickly learned that the approval of the crowd was fleeting and didn't matter much. What mattered was the approval of the coach. If I was to be useful to the team, I must follow the rules and please Coach Thimler.

*P*aul wrote to young Timothy, "No one serving as a soldier gets involved in civilian affairs—he wants to please his commanding officer" (2 Timothy 2:4). The righteous man realizes that the cheers of the crowd may bring fleeting happiness, but that the applause of the Lord is, in the end, the only applause that counts.

Trusting in my own mental understanding becomes
a hindrance to complete trust in God.

Oswald Chambers

You should not believe your conscience and
your feelings more than the word which the Lord
who receives sinners preaches to you.

Martin Luther

If God, like a father, denies us what we want now,
it is in order to give us some far better thing
later on. The will of God, we can rest assured,
is invariably a better thing.

Elisabeth Eliott

Today's Prayer

ord, Thank You for the affirmations of
my family and friends. But never let
me forget that Your approval is the
key to my life and my salvation.
Lord, I want to do Your will and to know
Your pleasure. Instruct me each day
that I might serve you with all that I am.

Amen

14

Help Me, Lord...

To Be a Man of Prayer

> "I want men everywhere to lift up
> holy hands in prayer…"
>
> *1 Timothy 2:8*

God wants men to pray. Prayer releases God's power and provision for successful Christian living. Yet too many of us don't pray as we ought. Why? Perhaps the act of prayer goes against the masculine need for independence (we men are notoriously slow to ask for help). Or perhaps we simply don't take the time needed to engage in a deep prayer relationship with God. But if we neglect our prayer lives, for whatever the reason, we forfeit one of God's great gifts to mankind.

Esther Burroughs worked with the Home Mission Board when she told me of the impact her father's prayer life had upon her. She recollected how each morning when she arose, she would walk down the hallway and pass the room where her father prayed. A crack in the door allowed her to witness a man of God engaged in sincere, devoted, life-changing conversation with the Master. All of us should be so fortunate as young Esther...and as wise as her father.

Prayer is God's provision for us to know Him,
to know His purposes and His ways, to experience
His mighty presence working in us and through
us to accomplish His perfect will.

Henry Blackaby

Does the Bible ever say anywhere from Genesis to
Revelation, "My house shall be called a house
of preaching?" Does it ever say, "My house shall
be called a house of music?" Of course not. The
Bible does say, "My house shall be called a house of
prayer for all nations." Preaching, music, the
reading of the Word—these things are fine; I believe
in and practice all of them. But they must never
override prayer as the defining mark of God's
dwelling. The honest truth is that I have seen God
do more in people's lives during ten minutes of
real prayer than in ten of my sermons.

Jim Cymbala

We must focus on prayer as the main thrust to
accomplish God's will and purpose on earth.
The forces against us have never been greater and
this is the only way we can release God's power
to become victorious.

John Maxwell

75

Today's Prayer

Lord, remind me that living this day
with You is infinitely better than going it alone.
As I acknowledge my dependence upon You,
I pray for all the things that You seek to
give me today so that I might do Your will
and live Your plan for my life. And for
whatever good I accomplish this day,
may You receive the glory.

Amen

Help Me, Lord...
To Have Endurance

"But you, man of God...
pursue endurance..."

1 Timothy 6:11

When I think of the word endurance, I think of my friend Larry Irving, 101 years young. Frail of body but keen of mind and humor, Larry is a joy to visit. I first met him and his wife when they were in their early seventies. At that time, Larry was recently retired from years of managing JC Penney stores, and his tireless work at our church raised my standard for servant leadership. Always willing to offer advice when asked, he did so with a gentleness and respect that required the listener to pay attention. And Larry backed up his words with a servant's spirit.

Larry is in a nursing home now. His sweet wife went on to her reward a few years ago. Sometimes when I visit Larry, he wonders out loud why he has been left here on this earth when he so desires to be with Jesus and his loving wife. Then, he tells me of the nurse he talked to about Jesus. Or he tells of the young man who works at the nursing home who prayed to receive Christ. Or he offers me advice on how to manage my business. Larry has many visitors, and we are all blessed beyond measure by this humble, righteous man.

Paul said it to Timothy (just as Larry has often said to me), "I have fought the good fight, I have finished the race, I have kept the faith. Now there is in store for me the crown of righteousness, which the Lord, the righteous Judge, will award to me on that day—and not only to me, but also to all who have longed for his appearing." (2 Timothy 4:7,8) But God still has work for Larry to do. Important work. And the same is true for you and me.

Keep adding, keep walking, keep advancing;
do not stop, do not turn back,
do not turn from the straight road.

St. Augustine

Let us not cease to do the utmost, that we may
incessantly go forward in the way of the Lord.

John Calvin

When the train goes through a tunnel and the
world gets dark, do you jump out? Of course not.
You sit still and trust the engineer
to get you through.

Corrie ten Boom

We have ample evidence that the Lord is able
to guide. The promises cover every imaginable
situation. All we need to do is to take the hand
He stretches out.

Elisabeth Eliott

Today's Prayer

*L*ord, Thank You for the years
You have given me and for the years
that I still have on this Earth. Help me to be
steadfast in my love and service for You.
May You find me faithful in all I do,
and may I finish the race joyfully and
then live with You forever.

Amen

Help Me, Lord...

To Be a Man of Noble Purposes

"In a large house there are articles not only of gold and silver, but also of wood and clay; some are for noble purposes and some for ignoble. If a man cleanses himself from the latter, he will be an instrument for noble purposes, made holy, useful to the Master and prepared to do any good work."

2 Timothy 2:20,21

I wasn't sure I had made the right decision taking my 13-year-old son to see the movie, "Saving Private Ryan." Having seen the movie alone a few weeks before, I was aware of its graphic details, but I was also aware of several strong messages I wanted my son to hear.

*O*n the ride home after the movie, Jimmy was talkative. One of the messages we discussed was the importance of picking one's personal battles. Some things, I said, are worth fighting for and many things aren't. Jimmy agreed.

*T*he righteous man knows which wars are worth fighting. The apostle Paul calls them "noble purposes." Certain causes are worthy of our attention, and certain things are better left undone. God's discernment is needed to know the important from the unimportant and the righteous from the unrighteous.

Oh Lord, let me not live to be useless.

John Wesley

God possesses infinite knowledge and an
awareness which is uniquely His. At all times,
even in the midst of any type of suffering, I can
realize that He knows, loves, watches, understands,
and more than that, He has a purpose.

Billy Graham

The beautiful thing about this adventure called
faith is that we can count on Him never to
lead us astray.

Charles Swindoll

Today's Prayer

*L*ord, there are many hands pulling at us.
Causes, many of which are worthy, demand
our time and attention. Help me, Lord,
to know the noble causes that You want me
to serve, and keep me always mindful of
Your purpose for my life.

Amen

Help Me, Lord...
To Walk With You

"Blessed is the man who does not walk in
the counsel of the wicked…"

Psalm 1:1

Be careful with whom you walk. Your associates will have a profound impact upon you. Your best walking partner is God. His conversation is always true and his advice is always right. Enoch walked with God and didn't die. (Genesis 5:24) I like to think that eventually, when they were walking, God said to Enoch, "We are closer to my house than yours. Come home with me."

When I was growing up, I knew a boy who acted like a chameleon. He took on the attitudes and values of those with whom he was walking. At church he could talk and act as spiritually as the next person. But at parties he could drink and tell off- color jokes as if he never went to church. He was swayed by those around him.

To some extent, we all are molded by our surroundings and our associates. But we also have the freedom to choose righteous walking partners, and it imperative that we do so: "…if we walk in the light, as he is in the light, we have fellowship with one another, and the blood of Jesus, his Son, purifies us from all sin." (1 John 1:7)

With whom will you walk today?

God is the beyond in the midst of our life.

Dietrich Bonhoeffer

Ask Christ to come into your heart to forgive
you and help you. When you do, Christ will take
up residence in your life by His Holy Spirit, and
when you face temptations and trials, you will no
longer face them alone.

Billy Graham

O God, Thou hast made us for thyself, and
ours hearts are restless until they find
their rest in Thee.

St. Augustine

Today's Prayer

*Lord, I am a mere man who can be tempted.
And I know that those who surround me
each day will influence me toward either
good or evil. Help me, Lord, to draw close to You,
and help me to claim righteous men and godly
women as my friends. Then, Lord,
I can walk fearlessly in the light of
Your counsel…and theirs.*

Amen

Help Me, Lord...
To Stand With You

> "Blessed is the man who does not...
> stand in the way of sinners..."
>
> *Psalm 1:1*

W*atch where you stand. Where you stand can be hazardous to your health. Once, while I was backpacking with friends along the Appalachian Trail, a powerful thunderstorm caught us by surprise. The rain came hard and cold as it stung our faces, but rain was the least of our worries. Lightning was striking all around us. Unfortunately we were hiking along a ridge top when the storm hit, so our options were both limited and dangerous. Where we decided to stand became a matter of life and death. We could stand under a tree on the ridge (very bad idea), or we could stand by a rock on the ridge (wet, cold, and exposed), or we could keep moving (which we did). Eventually, the storm passed.*

W here a man chooses to stand is a life-altering decision. If he chooses to stand with those who habitually sin, he will fall into their ways. If he stands with the ungodly, he will invite needless pain into his life. Standing with God, on the other hand, brings a man victory and joy.

L ike an experienced guide in a dangerous storm, God, leads the righteous man past the trials and temptations of this world. "No temptation has seized you except what is common to man. And God is faithful; he will not let you be tempted beyond what you can bear. But when you are tempted, he will also provide a way out so that you can stand up under it." (1 Corinthians 10:13) So watch where you stand.

Prayer plumes the wings of God's young eaglets
so that they may learn to mount above the clouds.
Prayer brings inner strength to God's warriors
and sends them forth to spiritual battle
with their muscles firm and
their armor in place.

C. H. Spurgeon

Every time you make a choice, you are turning
the central part of you, the part that chooses,
into something a little different from what
it was before.

C. S. Lewis

Today's Prayer

*L*ord, I want to stand with You today.
Guide my thoughts, my words, and my actions
to reflect the truth and goodness of a
loving God. And let me *take* a stand for You,
Lord, a stand for all to see. Let me be a
righteous, worthy ambassador for You
this day and every day.

Amen

19

Help Me, Lord...
To Sit With You

"Blessed is the man who does not...
sit is the seat of mockers..."

Psalm 1:1

The fact that you are reading this book indicates you have no intention of sitting with those who would make light of God or His creations. No Christian would purposely choose to mock God or to ignore Him, but sometimes we overlook God's presence, even when He sits in our midst.

Mary and Martha were entertaining Jesus at their home. Martha was busy fixing the meal and setting the table, all the while becoming more and more upset with Mary who had chosen instead to sit at the feet of Jesus and listen to Him. When Martha spoke to Jesus about Mary's apparent lack of effort, Jesus replied, "Martha, Martha, you are worried and upset about many things, but only one thing is needed. Mary has chosen what is better, and it will not be taken away from her." (Luke 10:38-42)

Martha did not intentionally slight Jesus—far from it. But the well-intentioned, hard-working Martha was mistaken when she chastised Mary. Mary, on the other hand, chose the right place to sit…at the feet of the Master. We should do likewise.

The beginning of anxiety is the end of faith,
and the beginning of true faith is
the end of anxiety.

George Mueller

Let your faith in Christ be in the quiet confidence
that He will every day and every moment keep
you as the apple of His eye, keep you in perfect
peace and in the sure experience of all the
light and the strength you need.

Andrew Murray

Begin to know Him now, and finish never.

Oswald Chambers

Today's Prayer

*L*ord, give me the discernment to know
when I am sitting with mockers, even
those with good intentions. I want to sit at
Your feet, Lord, and to be with *Your* people.
May all that I say and all that I do praise
and glorify Your name, and may
I sit at Your feet forever.

Amen

20

Help Me, Lord...

To Know the Joy of Living In You

> "I am the vine; you are the branches.
> If a man remains in me and I in him,
> he will bear much fruit; apart from me
> you can do nothing...I have told you this
> so that my joy may be in you and that
> your joy may be complete."
>
> *John 15:5,11*

*S*crubbing bathrooms at the Lutheran school was a radical change from my former life as a Congressional aide. God had called me to seminary, and His call had turned my life upside down. Only a few months before, I had rubbed shoulders with some of the most powerful men and women in the free world. I earned a good salary and enjoyed the perks of my profession. Now, the only thing perking was an occasional overflowing toilet. Now, I was rubbing shoulders with the hard end of a mop, and my janitor's paycheck seemed laughable. Yet now, I had never been happier or more at peace. I was where God wanted me to be. All the power, prestige, and possessions in the world could not buy the joy I felt being in the center of God's Will.

*T*he righteous man knows the source of true happiness. When it comes to genuine, deeply felt joy, the world makes empty promises, but God provides.

Feeling always seeks something in itself;
  faith keeps itself occupied with who Jesus is.
Do not forget that the faith of which God's Word
  speaks so much stands not only in opposition to
    works but also in opposition to feelings, and
therefore for a pure life of faith you must cease to
  seek your salvation not only in works but also in
    feelings. Let faith always speak against feeling.
When feeling says "In myself I am sinful, I am dark,
  I am weak, I am poor, I am sad," let faith say,
    "In Christ I am holy, I am light, I am strong,
      I am rich, I am joyful."

Andrew Murray

God loves you and wants you to experience
  peace and life—abundant and eternal.

Billy Graham

Do not let your happiness depend on something
  you may lose...only [upon] the Beloved who will
    never pass away.

C. S. Lewis

99

Today's Prayer

Lord, as Jesus abided in You
help me abide in Jesus. Remind me
that without You, I can do nothing.
Nothing in this world compares to You, Lord.
May my joy be complete as
I give my life to You.

Amen

21

Help Me, Lord...

Present My Faith
with
Gentleness and Respect

"…Always be prepared to give an answer
to everyone who asks you to give the
reason for the hope that you have. But
do this with gentleness and respect…
1 Peter 3:15

*R*on Medlin and I are friends. And I sometimes wonder why. Our philosophies of life, our politics, and our views on religion are often at odds. Ron tends to approve of the liberal slant while I fall into the conservative category. Ron presents his views without hesitation, so I always know how he feels about a given topic, and he presents his opinions with strength, clarity, and undeniable conviction. Still, I often disagree with him, albeit respectfully.

*T*hough Ron and I may debate theology and politics, we are still close friends. I can hear Ron's point of view because I know it is rooted in a caring and concern for the well-being of mankind. And behind the vigor and force of his viewpoint is a gentleness and respect for my opposing opinions.

*T*he righteous man has a strong commitment to the truth. He is commanded by God to share that truth with family, friends, and the world. Christian men can and should support each other even when they disagree. Sometimes, God places friends along our paths to correct faulty thoughts or lapses in judgement. Maybe this is why God placed me in Ron's path. Or, maybe this is why God placed Ron in mine. Or maybe, just maybe, God has something to teach both of us.

We can never have more of true faith than
we have of true humility.

Andrew Murray

The Christian is not one who has gone all the
way with Christ. None of us has. The Christian is
one who has found the right road.

Charles L. Allen

No receipt opens the heart but a true friend,
to whom you may impart griefs, joys, fears,
fears, hopes, suspicions, counsels, and
whatever lies upon the heart.

Francis Bacon

I look upon all the world as my parish.

John Wesley

Today's Prayer

ord, You have given me a hope that transcends the daily grind and the difficult circumstances of life. Because of Your Son Jesus, I can face this day with assurance and joy. Help me, Lord, to share that hope with the friends I meet along the way. Let my convictions be expressed strongly but with a gentleness and respect. And help me to be open to the genuine concerns and opinions of godly friends.

Amen

Help Me, Lord...

To Be an Overcomer

Jesus answered, "I have told you these things, so that in me you may have peace. In this world you will have trouble. But take heart! I have overcome the world."

John 16:33

If you go to the Sunday morning service at the Baptist church in Leiper's Fork, Tennessee, you'll be greeted at the front door with a big smile, a bulletin, and a handshake compliments of Jim Pewitt. Jim and his wife Lois are among the most faithful attendees of our little church. On Sunday evenings and Wednesday nights, the Pewitts are always present and accounted for. The same goes for Vacation Bible School, revivals, and special events—Jim and Lois always give their full support.

The remarkable part of this story is that Jim has no voice. Several years ago, surgery left him without the ability to speak, and nothing to show for it but a hole in his throat and a voice box in his pocket. But that little setback couldn't wipe the smile off Jim's face for long.

Some days Jim just doesn't feel very well, but you'll never hear him complain. And on Sunday morning, rain or shine, Jim will be right there at the doors of the church with a smile on his face and a stack of bulletins under his arm. On Wednesday evenings, he even gives the prayer at our prayer meetings. Jim Pewitt is not just a good man, and he's not just an ambassador for God. He is also an "overcomer."

Jesus overcame the troubles of this world. He said we, too, would have trouble, but He told us not to worry. As Christians, we can still have peace in our lives—even under difficult circumstances—because of our Savior. Armed with the good news of Christ Jesus, Christians overcome the inevitable trials and tribulations of this life. Just like Jim Pewitt.

We must face today as children of tomorrow.
We must meet the uncertainties of this world
with the certainty of the world to come.
To the pure in heart, nothing really bad
can happen... not death but sin
should be our great fear.

A.W. Tozer

God of our life, there are days when the burdens
we carry chafe our shoulders and weigh us down;
when the road seems dreary and endless, the skies
grey and threatening; when our lives have no music
in them, and our hearts are lonely, and our souls have
lost their courage. Flood the path with light,
run our eyes to where the skies are full of promise;
tune our hearts to brave music; give us the
sense of comradeship with heroes and saints of
every age; and so quicken our spirits that we
may be able to encourage the souls of all who
journey with us on the road of life,
to Your honour and glory.

St. Augustine

Today's Prayer

*L*ord, Thank You for Jesus.
He lived in this same world that I live in
and faced numerous troubles, just like me.
Because He overcame the difficulties of this life,
so can I. Help me look to Jesus when difficulties
come my way so that I, too, might overcome my
troubles, and, in doing so, be a model for others
and an ambassador for You.

Amen

23

Help Me, Lord...
To Delight in Your Word

> "But his delight is in the law of the LORD…"
>
> *Psalm 1:2a*

King David writes that a man will find happiness and great blessings if he studies God's Word and obeys His laws. David advises, "Delight yourself in the LORD and he will give you the desires of your heart." *(Psalm 37:4)*

Jesus says "blessed is the man who hungers and thirsts after righteousness, for he will be filled."*(Matthew 5:6)* Righteousness is found in God's Word, but God does not force his teachings upon us. God gives man the ability to choose between the joys of righteous living and the temptations of the world. The world offers opportunities for pleasure which soon evaporate like mist at daybreak. God, on the other hand, offers fulfillment. And abundance. And joy. And eternal life.

Today, you can choose to delight in the Lord, or not. You can read his Word, or not. You can accept His blessings, or not. God offers freely, and the righteous man accepts God's gifts with thanksgiving and delight.

What, then, is the Bible? It is the Book of Life.
"The words that I speak unto you," said our Lord,
"they are spirit, and they are life."

A.W. Tozer

If I find in myself a desire which no experience in
this world can satisfy, the most probable
explanation is that I was made
for another world.

C.S. Lewis

The Bible is God's Word, given to us by God
Himself so we can know Him and
His will for our lives.

Billy Graham

Voltaire expected that within fifty years of his
lifetime, there would not be one Bible in the
world. His house is now a distribution center for
Bibles in many languages.

Corrie ten Boom

Today's Prayer

*L*ord, I want to delight in You and
Your Word. Help me to make the time and
take the time to study the Bible. Increase my
thirst for You and Your righteousness,
and always keep me mindful that it is
through Your blessings that I will
achieve lasting peace.

Amen

24

Help Me, Lord...
To Meditate on
Your Word

> "...and on his law he meditates
> day and night."
>
> *Psalm 1:2b*

*M*editation doesn't come easy for many of us, and it certainly doesn't come easy for me. A seemingly endless string of urgent demands cries out for my time, sometimes leaving precious few moments for communion with God. Sometimes, when the noise of life becomes deafening, I am reminded of a small trailer that I called home while I attended seminary.

*T*he campus of New Orleans Baptist Theological Seminary is located on the busy Gentilly Boulevard thoroughfare, close to an industrial barge canal, not far from a small but busy airport, and within yards of bustling train tracks. One night I lay in bed, exhausted from a non-stop day of classes, study, and work. As I closed my eyes, a train came roaring down the tracks rattling the foundation of my trailer with a decibel count akin to that of a tornado. After the train passed, I listened to the sirens of emergency vehicles racing down Gentilly Boulevard. Soon, the tugboats were blowing their air horns requesting the bridge keeper to raise the bridge. And the private jets sounded like they were performing an air show. My little world was noisy indeed, but whenever I slowed down and quietly sought God, even amid the hustle and bustle, He was there.

*W*e live in a world of non-stop action and noise. We become desensitized to the need for rest and quietness. Sometimes, we become restless when faced with a few moments of free time or a few moments of solitude. Yet, we need these moments of stillness in order to successfully navigate the journey of life. "Be still, and know that I am God…," admonishes the Psalmist. (Psalm 46:10a) After Jesus spent a long, busy day teaching, casting out demons, and healing *the sick, He rested. And the scripture records, "Very early in the morning, while it was still dark, Jesus got up, left the house and went off to a solitary place, where he prayed." (Mark 1:35)*

The righteous man needs meditation. God can speak any way He chooses, but most often, He speaks in a still, soft voice. Only when we find a way to turn off the noise and close off the clutter do we fully appreciate the presence and peace of the Lord.

The remedy for distractions is the same now as
it was in earlier and simpler times: prayer,
meditation, and the cultivation of the inner life.

A.W. Tozer

The main thing that God asks for is our attention.

Jim Cymbala

I have so much to do that I shall spend the
first three hours in prayer.

Martin Luther

115

Today's Prayer

*L*ord, slow me down. Help me never to
let the urgent crowd out the important.
Let me guard my time and order my day so
that I might always spend time with You.
Knowing You and Your Word is the most
important item on my agenda this day.
And the busier I am, the more time I
need to spend with You.

Amen

25

Help Me, Lord...

To Be a Man of Integrity

> "The man of integrity walks securely,
> but he who takes crooked paths
> will be found out."
>
> *Proverbs 10:9*

*A*fter four years in the United States Air Force, I went back to college and majored in political science. During that time, I was extremely fortunate to secure a job with U. S. Representative, James Haley. As a congressional aide, I was able to make practical application of the theory I was learning in school. I learned politics from my boss, of course, but I learned something else, something much more important: integrity.

*T*he congressman was a stickler for doing things right. When I opened his district office, he made it very clear that he expected everything that we did or said in his name to be above reproach. For example, he was a stickler when it came to the use of the franking privilege (franking is the name for the free postage that is afforded members of Congress and the Executive Office when they send mail on "official" business). Some House members abused this privilege, but never Mr. Haley. He purchased stamps from his own funds and handed them to me with crystal-clear instructions: If I had any questions about whether or not the post was government business, I was to use the congressman's stamps. Period.

*R*epresentative Haley was a man of integrity who used his position of power to influence his employees and constituents to do the right thing. And for him, doing the right thing wasn't an abstract concept—it started with the man in the mirror and then worked its way out from there. You and I should do no less. Period.

In the worst temptations, nothing can help us
but faith that God's Son has put on flesh, is bone,
sits at the right hand of the Father, and prays for us.
There is no mightier comfort.

Martin Luther

When we choose deliberately to obey Him,
then He will tax the remotest star and the
last grain of sand to assist us with all
His almighty power.

Oswald Chambers

We have a God who delights in impossibilities.

Andrew Murray

Today's Prayer

*L*ord, there is no temptation I will face
today You have not already seen and
conquered. May I know Your presence and
discernment in all my choices.
And may everything I say and do reflect
an integrity that is pleasing in Your sight.

Amen

26

Help Me, Lord...

To Find My Rest in You

"Are you tired? Worn out? Burned out on
religion? Come to me. Get away with
me and you'll recover your life. I'll show
you how to take a real rest. Walk with
me and work with me, watch how I do it.
Learn the unforced rhythms of grace. I
won't lay anything heavy or ill-fitting on
you. Keep company with me and you'll
learn to live freely and lightly."

Matthew 11:28-30 THE MESSAGE

One Sunday morning, I stopped preaching and started meddling. Using humor and personal examples, I spoke of how it feels to pontificate from the pulpit while someone in the congregation falls into deep (and I do mean deep) slumber. After sharing my thoughts with the congregation, I moved on to more acceptable topics.

As I stood shaking hands after the service, I had almost forgotten my brief foray into meddling when one of my saintly church members made an interesting observation. He said that when one slept in church, it meant that he was at peace with God. Perhaps the church member was right...in some cases, but sometimes, sleeping in church on Sunday morning probably reflects too much Saturday night. But I digress.

The desire to find peace with God is a deep human need. Jesus promises that we can find that peace when we come to Him. Jesus teaches us to about the "unforced rhythms of grace," and He promises that with Him, we can "learn to live freely and lightly." When we do, we can then enter God's house with a sense of peace that will allow us to joyfully praise His name and listen to His word ...with eyes open, please.

Worry does not empty tomorrow of its sorrow;
  it empties today of its strength.

Corrie ten Boom

Christ alone can bring lasting peace —
    peace with God —
  peace among men and nations —
    and peace within our hearts.

Billy Graham

Anxiety has its use, stimulating us to seek with
  keener longing for that security where peace is
    complete and unassailable.

St. Augustine

Pray, and let God worry.

Martin Luther

Today's Prayer

*L*ord, Thank You for the rest You provide. Help me to walk with You each day and enjoy the peace that is found only in relationship to You. And may I always be ready to share Your peace with everyone whom I meet, and may I always give You the praise and the glory.

Amen

27

Help Me, Lord...

To Be Productive
and
Responsible

> "For even when we were with you,
> we gave this rule:
> 'If a man will not work,
> he shall not eat.'"
>
> *2 Thessalonians 3:10*

Everyone wants freedom, but not everyone wants responsibility. "Liberty" is a grand, high-sounding word with lots of pomp and circumstance. "Responsibility," on the other hand, sounds a lot like work. The irony is this: Liberty and responsibility, while seemingly disparate concepts, are inexorably related. There can be no lasting liberty without responsibility.

In a society where too many men wish to pass blame (and work) off to others, the righteous man does neither. Instead, he accepts responsibility for his own behavior and for the support of his family. The righteous man never abuses his own personal freedoms. Instead, he works diligently, cares for his family, and contributes to his church and his community.

Paul writes to the Thessalonians that a man eats if he works. Simple enough. And true. The Bible encourages each of us to take full responsibility for ourselves, for our actions, and for our families. When we do, we not only please God, but we also leave a lasting legacy for those we love.

Freedom is not an absence of responsibility;
   but rather a reward we receive when we've
   performed our responsibility with excellence.

Charles Swindol

We trust as if it all depended on God,
   and work as if it all depended on us.

C. H. Spurgeon

Ordinary work, which is what most of us do most
   of the time, is ordained by God every bit
   as much as is the extraordinary.

Elisabeth Elliot

If God is diligent, surely we ought to be diligent in
doing our duty to Him. Think how patient and
diligent God has been to us!

Oswald Chambers

Today's Prayer

*L*ord, Thank You for the health and abilities You have provided me. Help me to use all Your gifts to work diligently so that I might provide for my family and give generously to others. May I always be a dedicated Christian and a responsible member of Your kingdom here on earth.

Amen

Help Me, Lord...

To Pursue
Righteousness

> "But you, man of God,
> pursue righteousness…"
>
> *1 Timothy 6:11*

A. W. Tozer writes, "No man should desire to be happy who is not at the same time holy. He should spend his efforts in seeking to know and do the will of God, leaving to Christ the matter of how happy he shall be." But often, we are tempted to seek happiness first and righteousness second, with decidedly *unhappy* results.

The righteous man does not chase blindly after happiness. As a mature Christian, he understands that joy is not a destination that can be reached directly, but that it is a byproduct of righteous living and communion with God.

When we live according to God's laws, we find fulfillment, abundance, and, ultimately, joy. In fact, joy is one of the many gifts that God bestows upon his children, and He stands forever ready to deliver those gifts at the same instant His children are ready—and willing—to accept them.

Impurity is not just a wrong action;
impurity is the state of mind and heart
and soul which is just the opposite of
purity and wholeness.

A.W. Tozer

It is quite true to say, "I can't live a holy life,"
but you can decide to let Jesus make you holy.

Oswald Chambers

Resolved, never to do anything which
I should be afraid to do if it were the
last hour of my life.

Jonathan Edwards

Never support an experience which does not
have God as its source, and
faith in God as its result.

Oswald Chambers

131

Today's Prayer

*L*ord, help me to approach this day with
a deep sense of respect for Your word and for
Your laws. Help me to live righteously,
courageously, and purely. Keep me mindful
of my responsibilities, keep me humble of spirit,
keep me thankful for my blessings. Help me,
Lord, to see your way more clearly today, and
help me to live according to Your will.

Amen

Help Me, Lord...
To Pursue Faith

"But you, man of God,
pursue faith…"

1 Timothy 6:11

Dwight L. Moody once observed, "There are three kinds of faith in Christ: First, a struggling faith, like a man in deep water desperately swimming. Second, a clinging faith, like a man hanging to the side of a boat. But there is also a third kind of faith, a resting faith, like a man safely within the boat. That man can then reach out with a hand to help someone else get in."

Moody understood that mature Christians feel the deep sense of security that God offers His children. But he also understood that from time to time, even dedicated Christians can feel overwhelmed by their circumstances.

To maintain the "resting" faith that Moody describes, we must make our communion with God an everyday occurrence. We must visit Him often in prayer and seek His wisdom through the regular reading of His Word. We must worship Him and tell the world about His Son. When we do, God sends us His grace and His peace which we, in turn, can share with the world.

The beginning of anxiety is the end of faith,
and the beginning of true faith is
the end of anxiety.

George Mueller

Faith does not struggle; faith lets God do it all.

Corrie ten Boom

The whole being of any Christian is
Faith and Love...
Faith brings the man to God,
love brings him to men.

Martin Luther

Faith in God is a terrific venture in the dark.

Oswald Chambers

Today's Prayer

*L*ord, sometimes I am plagued by worry and doubt. Help me always to understand that genuine faith in You means that I can release my fears and depend upon You for my deliverance. Help me to do those things that will strengthen my faith, and help me to always trust in You as I seek Your wisdom and Your will.

Amen

30

Help Me, Lord...
To Pursue Love

God is love and the righteous man is to be a reflection of that love to a needy world. How should that love manifest itself in our lives? Paul answers that question when he writes to the church at Corinth:

> Love never gives up.
> Love cares more for others than for self.
> Love doesn't want what it doesn't have.
> Love doesn't strut,
> Doesn't have a swelled head,
> Doesn't force itself on others,
> Isn't always "me first,"
> Doesn't fly off the handle,
> Doesn't keep score of the sins of others,
> Doesn't revel when others grovel,
> Takes pleasure in the flowering of truth,
> Puts up with anything,
> Trusts God always,
> Always looks for the best,
> Never looks back,
> But keeps going to the end.

I Corinthians 13:4-8 The Message

Love is…a steady wish for the loved person's
ultimate good….

C. S. Lewis

He who is filled with love is filled with God Himself.

St. Augustine

Give me such love for God and men as will
blot out all hatred and bitterness.

Dietrich Bonhoeffer

Today's Prayer

*L*ord, Your love for me is more
than I could possibly deserve. Your love is
transforming. Let me never forget
Your love for me, let me never cease in
praising You, and use me this day to reflect
Your love to all those whom I meet.

Amen

31

Help Me, Lord...

To Pursue Gentleness

> "But you, man of God...
> pursue gentleness…"
>
> *1 Timothy 6:11*

*S*omehow gentleness has become a trait most men are not interested in. Perhaps the idea of "self-made man" seems incompatible with gentleness. If that be the case, the definition of gentleness needs revisiting. Among the synonyms for gentleness, the word "broken" is found: as in a broken horse. In this sense, "broken" means strength under control.

*"T*he Horse Whisperer," a good book and movie, tells about a cowboy who tames wild horses with firmness, soft words, and patience. Initially, his horses are strong and powerful but out of control. When the cowboy is finished, his horses are still strong and beautiful, but they are also controllable and useful.

*T*he righteous man understands that gentleness is not a sign of weakness. A gentle spirit is a sign of strength under control. Paul writes that gentleness is part of the makeup of a righteous man filled with God's spirit. (Galatians 5:22) Followers of Christ are both strong and gentle. The righteous man controls himself and focuses his energies on the work of God's kingdom. And when he does, God smiles.

We can always gauge where we are by the
teachings of Jesus Christ.

Oswald Chambers

It is the duty of every Christian to be
Christ to his neighbor.

Martin Luther

Since you cannot do good to all, you are to pay
special regard to those who, by the
accidents of time, or place, or circumstances,
are brought into closer connection with you.

St. Augustine

Today's Prayer

*L*ord, don't let the world define
what kind of man I should be.
May I turn to Your Word for my guidance.
Let me be sure and strong in purpose and in will,
yet gentle in demeanor.

Amen

*Selected Bible Verses
by Topic*

GOD LEADS US TOWARD RIGHTEOUSNESS AND REWARDS US WHEN WE FOLLOW HIS PATH

Blessings crown the head of the righteous, but
   violence overwhelms the mouth of the wicked.

Proverbs 10:6 NIV

The steps of a good man are ordered by
               the LORD....

Psalm 37:23 KJV

Blessed are those who hunger and thirst for
   righteousness, for they will be filled.

Matthew 5:6 NIV

...the path of the just is as the shining light, that
   shineth more and more unto the perfect day.
       The way of the wicked is as darkness:
       they know not at what they stumble.

Proverbs 4:18-19 KJV

Victory comes from you, O Lord.
       May your blessings rest on your people.

Psalm 3:8 NLT

146

WHEN WE BEHAVE RIGHTEOUSLY, GOD SMILES

Teach me your ways, O Lord, that I may live
according to your truth! Grant me purity of heart,
that I may honor you.

Psalm 86:11 NLT

He who sows wickedness reaps trouble.

Proverbs 22:8 NIV

For the Lord God is our light and our protector.
He gives us grace and glory. No good thing will
the Lord withhold from those who do what is right.
O Lord Almighty, happy are those who trust in you.

Psalm 84: 11-12 NLT

Let us walk honestly, as in the day; not in rioting
and drunkenness, not in chambering and
wantonness, not in strife and envying.

Romans: 13:13 KJV

Jesus answered and said unto him, If a man love me,
he will keep my words: and my Father will
love him, and we will come unto him,
and make our abode with him.

John 14:23 KJV

HAVE FAITH IN TOMORROW,
HAVE FAITH IN GOD

Surely goodness and mercy shall follow me all
the days of my life: and I will dwell in the house of
the Lord for ever.

Psalm 23:6 KJV

But he must ask in faith without any doubting,
for the one who doubts is like the surf of the sea,
driven and tossed by the wind.

James 1:6 NASB

Take therefor no thought for the morrow:
for the morrow shall take thought for the things of
itself. Sufficient unto the day is the evil thereof.

Matthew 6:34 KJV

Be on the alert, stand firm in the faith,
act like men, be strong.

I Corinthians 16:13 NASB

For the Lord watches over the way of the righteous,
but the way of the wicked will perish.

Psalm 1:6 NIV

THE POWER OF FAITH

… for truly I say to you, if you have faith as a
mustard seed, you shall say to this mountain,
"Move from here to there" and it shall move; and
nothing shall be impossible to you.

Matthew 17:20 NASB

In thee, O Lord, do I put my trust;
let me never be put into confusion.

Psalm 71:1 KJV

Trust in him at all times, O people; pour out
your hearts to him, for God is our refuge.

Psalm 62:8 NIV

The Lord's lovingkindnesses indeed never cease,
for His compassions never fail. They are new
every morning. Great is Thy faithfulness.

Lamentations 3:22-23 NASB

For in the gospel a righteousness is being revealed,
a righteousness that is by faith from first to last,
just as it is written:
"The righteous will live by faith."

Romans 1:17 NIV

WORSHIP GOD WITH
A JOYFUL HEART

These things have I spoken unto you,
        that my joy might remain in you,
        and that your joy might be full.

John 15:11 KJV

Rejoice evermore. Pray without ceasing.
        In every thing give thanks: for this is the will
        of God in Christ Jesus concerning you.

I Thessalonians 5:16-18 KJV

You will show me the way of life, granting me the
        joy of your presence and the pleasures of
        living with you forever.

Psalm 16:11 NLT

Delight thyself also in the LORD;
        and he shall give thee the desires of thine heart.

Psalm 37:4 KJV

Rejoice, and be exceeding glad:
        for great is your reward in heaven....

Matthew 5:12 KJV

TODAY IS GOD"S GIFT
LET US REJOICE AND GIVE THANKS

This is the day the Lord has made;
　　　let us rejoice and be glad in it.

Psalm 118:24 NIV

...let the hearts of those who seek the Lord rejoice.
　　　Look to the Lord and his strength;
　　　　seek his face always.

I Chronicles 16:10-11 NIV

The Lord is king! Let the earth rejoice!
　　　Let the farthest islands be glad.

Psalm 97:1 NLT

These things I have spoken unto you, that in me
　　　ye might have peace. In the world ye shall
　　　have tribulation: but be of good cheer;
　　　　I have overcome the world.

John 16:33 KJV

It is good to give thanks to the Lord, to sing praises
　　　to the Most High. It is good to proclaim your
　　　unfailing love in the morning
　　　your faithfulness in the evening.

Psalm 92:2-3 NLT

GOD CALLS UPON US
TO SHOW KINDNESS TO OTHERS

Be ye therefore merciful, as your Father also
is merciful.

Luke 6:36 KJV

A kind man benefits himself,
but a cruel man brings trouble on himself.

Proverbs 11:17 NIV

A gentle answer turns away wrath,
but a harsh word stirs up anger.

Proverbs 15:1 NIV

A new commandment I give unto you,
That ye love one another; as I have loved you....

John 13:34 KJV

...Verily I say unto you, Inasmuch as ye have done
it unto one of the least of these my brethren,
ye have done it unto me.

Matthew 25:40 KJV

GOD'S PEACE

And let the peace of God rule in your hearts
and be ye thankful.

Colossians 3:15 KJV

Be perfect, be of good comfort, be of one mind,
live in peace; and the God of love and
peace shall be with you.

II Corinthians 13:11 KJV

Return unto thy rest, O my soul; for the
LORD hath dealt bountifully with thee.

Psalm 116:7 KJV

Come to me all you who are weary and burdened,
and I will give you rest. Take my yoke upon you
and learn from me, for I am gentle and humble in
heart, and you will find rest for your soul. For my
yoke is easy and my burden is light.

Matthew 11:28-30 NIV

Peace I leave with you, my peace I give unto you:
not as the world giveth, give I unto you.
Let not your heart be troubled,
neither let it be afraid.

John 14:27 KJV

THE POWER OF PRAYER

In my distress I called upon the Lord;
I cried unto my God for help.
From his temple, he heard my voice.

Psalm 18:6 NIV

I sought the Lord, and he heard me,
and delivered me from all my fears.

Psalm 34:4 KJV

...for your Father knows what you need,
before you ask Him.

Matthew 6:8 NASB

Ask and it shall be given to you; seek and you shall
find; knock and it shall be opened to you.
For every one who asks receives, and he who seeks
finds, and to him who knocks it shall be opened.

Matthew 7:7 NASB

Cast your burden upon the Lord and He will
sustain you: He will never allow the
righteous to be shaken.

Psalm 55:22 NASB

WHEN QUESTIONS ARISE,
PRAYER IS THE ANSWER

In the day of my trouble I shall call upon Thee,
  for Thou wilt answer me.

Psalm 86:7 NASB

And it will come about that whoever calls on
  the name of the Lord will be delivered.

Joel 2:32 NASB

The Lord is far from the wicked but he hears
  the prayer of the righteous.

Proverbs 15:29 NIV

...Our Father which art in heaven,
  Hallowed be thy name. Thy kingdom come,
  Thy will be done in earth, as it is in heaven.

Matthew 6:9-10 KJV

Watch ye therefore, and pray always....

Luke 21:36

WHEN WE SEEK GOD'S BLESSINGS AND DISCOVER HIS PLAN, WE SUCCEED

Success, success to you, and success to those
who help you, for your God is with you....

I Chronicles 12:18 NIV

The God of heaven, he will prosper us;
therefore we his servants will arise and build...

Nehemiah 2:20 KJV

Who are those who fear the Lord? He will
show them the path they should choose.
They will live in prosperity, and their children will
inherit the Promised Land.

Psalm 25:12-13 NLT

For the Lord God is our light and our protector.
He gives us grace and glory. No good thing will the
Lord withhold from those who do what is right.
O Lord Almighty, happy are those who trust in you.

Psalm 84: 11-12 NLT

But son, do not forget my teaching, but keep my
commandments in your heart, for they will prolong
your life many years and bring you prosperity.

Proverbs 3:1-2 NIV

TRUSTING GOD

Trust the Lord your God with all your heart and
lean not on your own understanding; in all your
ways acknowledge him, and he will
make your paths straight.

Proverbs 3:5-6 NIV

The Lord says, "I will guide you along the best
pathway for your life. I will advise you and
watch over you."

Psalm 32:8 NLT

Submit yourselves therefore to God.
Resist the devil, and he will flee from you.
Draw nigh to God, and he will draw nigh to you.

James 4:7-8 KJV

The LORD is my rock, and my fortress,
and my deliverer; my God, my strength,
in whom I will trust....

Psalm 18:2 KJV

Commit everything you do to the Lord.
Trust him, and he will help you.

Psalm 37:5 NLT

GOD CALLS UPON US TO HAVE AN OPTIMISTIC, COURAGEOUS, FAITH-INSPIRED ATTITUDE

I can do everything through him that
gives me strength.

Phillippians 4:13 NIV

The Lord is my light and my salvation;
whom shall I fear? The Lord is the strength of
my life; of whom shall I be afraid?

Psalm 27:1 KJV

Be of good courage, and he shall strengthen your
heart, all ye that hope in the Lord.

Psalm 31:24 KJV

These things have I spoken unto you, that my joy
might remain in you, and that your joy might be full.

John 15:11 KJV

Finally, brethren, whatsoever things are true,
whatsoever things are honest, whatsoever things
are just, whatsoever things are pure, whatsoever
things are lovely, whatsoever things are of
good report; if there be any virtue, and if
there be any praise, think on these things.

Phillippians 4:8 KJV

About the Author

Jim Gallery lives and writes in Middle Tennessee. He serves as senior editor for both Brighton Books and Walnut Grove Press. In addition, Jim is a sought-after speaker and lecturer. He also has 20 year's experience as a pastor.

Jim is a graduate of the University of South Florida and the New Orleans Baptist Theological Seminary. He is the father of two children.

Some of his other titles include:

God Can Handle It
God Can Handle It... Teenagers
Prayers of a Godly Woman
Prayers of a Dedicated Teacher